I0469759

Photography

A Comprehensive Guide To Capturing Stunning Digital Photos

Introduction

Photography is one of the most fulfilling, creative, lucrative and challenging art forms. While recording images for posterity has been practiced since ancient times and only by a select few, the modern age and its technology have allowed photography to be the hobby for everybody. No other technology has made photography more accessible than the digital camera.

While cameras come in all shapes, sizes, cost and capacity, digital cameras have the potential to turn any novice photographer seem like an expert with a couple of adjustments. Any advanced photographer will admit that digital cameras are still one of the best tools for them and their less experienced hobbyists. Whether you are a beginner or an expert photographer, digital cameras can be one of your best and even indispensable choices.

While photography is art, there are still scientific rules that apply to its expression. While the artistic side of photography can be achieved by the photographer's creativity, passion and personal expression, the technical side has to be learned. Only when the nuts and bolts of a camera are fully learned can a photographer maximize their tools to its fullest potential. When creativity merges together with technology, the results can truly be one of the most inspiring, provoking and most importantly memorable art pieces in life.

This comprehensive guide will provide you with the whole gamut of photography. It presents you with a range of basic topics for the beginners and advanced or special topics for the expert. From the basic parts of your camera to often overlooked features, from a brief overview of photography to the modern tips and trends of photography today and from one sample after another to show you the applications of major photography lessons, this book definitely has something for every photography aficionado.

Topics in this guide are:

Basics: How Your Camera Works
Camera Equipment & Accessories
Camera Lenses
Photography Techniques
Composition
Special Topics

While there may be hundreds of digital camera models, most of them have basically the same parts and functions. For the instructional purposes of this guide, a Nikon camera has been used to describe the location of every major component in the camera. Most of the time, the parts and the features will also be approximately the same as with other models and manufacturers. As you may know, the better or more state of the art the camera is, the better its clarity and functionality become. The features and functions discussed in this guide represent the general capabilities found in the average digital camera. The camera you have may share the same features but it may have different levels of capacities.

For the best learning experience, it is recommended that you hold your camera as you read this guide. For every chapter about a specific part, feature or photography tip, apply it immediately. You can learn faster and retain the lesson longer when you pair reading with application.

Table of Contents

Chapter Four: Photography Techniques

Chapter Five: Composition

Chapter One: Basics: How Your Camera Works

Understanding Digital Camera Sensors

The camera sensor is the soul of the camera body. It is where light is collected and captured, then converted and processed to an image. Comparing to human anatomy, the sensor works as the retina, where light is focused by the lens and an image is processed and perceived in the brain. This works the same with camera sensors, as light is being focused on it after the shutter curtain opens. It is the function of the lens to properly focus the light on the sensor, then, sensor processes the image.

Camera sensors come in different sizes and it dictates the size of camera body. The sensor size has bearing on the quality of the image created. In a bigger camera sensor, light receptors captures more light, generating a stronger electrical signal, thus creating a better image. If you have two camera bodies with different sensor size but with the same pixel count, the bigger camera sensor will produce a better quality image than that of the smaller counterpart.

Photo receptors, also known as Pixels these days, are larger on the much bigger camera sensor. The key function of these photo receptors is to receive light, and then it would generate an electrical signal that is converted into a digital image signal. More light means stronger image signal.

Bigger camera sensors come with a hefty price tag, but it is a good investment. It is the most expensive component of the camera system. Nowadays, big players are working their way to keep on improving their sensors. The better the processor, the faster it renders the image and the better quality of the photograph.

As with other electronic devices, the sensor is the most important and most sensitive part of the camera. It should be kept clean as any dust particles lodged on the sensor will create a speck on the image. In the event the camera sensor had particles lodged, do not attempt to clean it yourself if you are not expert on it, then it is recommended to have it checked and cleaned by a camera expert.

Understanding Camera Exposure: Aperture, ISO and Shutter Speed

In photography, Exposure is defined as the amount of light that gets through the camera system. The three camera settings that can only affect the exposure of your picture would be the Aperture, ISO sensitivity and Shutter Speed. Each setting has its own variables and affects the other settings. These settings apply to every camera – even camera on smart phones. Any change that you make to any of the settings, you are changing them by units called "stops". You need to adjust one step up or down to either halve or double the amount of lights that goes through the camera system.
The exposure can be maintained by compensating with one of the other two setting. The capacity to balance the three settings means you can expose the picture properly with a number of combinations, but may look minimally different to each other.

The aperture is the hole within the lens diaphragm. It controls the amount of light that enters the lens and it also controls the depth of field which is explained later.

ISO speed is related to sensitivity to light of the camera sensor. The higher the value, the more sensitive the camera sensor is, the brighter the image is created. ISO is also the digital equivalent of film speed. A digital camera changes the ISO sensitivity by pumping more electricity to the image sensor. The dark side of having a high ISO value is the appearance of image noise.

Shutter speed is related to the amount of time the camera sensor is exposed to light. The faster the shutter speed, the less light enters and can be used to stop or freeze any motion. The slower the shutter speed, more light enters, the brighter the exposure. If something is in motion while the shutter is open, you can get what they call motion blur. Shutter speed setting is measured in seconds or fractions of a second such as ½ second, 1/200 seconds and 1/500 seconds.

Setting for handheld photography is 1/100 second or 1/160 second. If you are steady enough, you can get away with a shutter speed as low as 1/40 second with the same quality of the image.

Understanding Camera Metering

Metering is the brains on how the camera determines the shutter speed and aperture based on the lighting conditions or amount of light that enters the camera. It is critical for the photographer or camera user to understand how the camera meters the light to achieve photographs with consistent and accurate exposure.

Most DSLR's have three common modes which are Matrix Metering, Center Weighted Metering and Spot Metering. Each of these metering modes has its own set of advantage and disadvantage in every lighting situation. Understanding how this metering modes work would help improve one's photographic perception.

Matrix metering or Evaluative metering – By default, this mode meters the light levels in the entire frame and would try to come up with a balanced bright and darks areas of the image. This metering mode is the default setting on most DSLRs these days.

Center Weighted – reading takes place on the center of the image. It is not always desirable to meter the entire image in determining the correct exposure. This can be used in portraiture if your subject is placed on the center of the frame.

Spot Metering – the camera meters on the specified focus point and ignores everything else within the frame. This mode is perfect for subject that does not take big space within the frame and you want to achieve a good exposure of it. You can use with a subject that is backlit or you want to achieve a silhouette image.

Understanding Depth of Field

The Depth of Field (DoF) denotes the sharpness of the foreground, subject and background or the range of distance that appears adequately sharp. The depth of field does not abruptly change from sharp to not sharp, but a gradual transition.
Large depth of field renders all the elements of photograph in focus or in detail. It is commonly used in landscape photography where details from all elements of the image are needed. It is obtained by having a small aperture.

A Shallow depth of field renders a blurry part of the image, where the foreground and background can be isolated to each other. This is used usually in portraiture, where the photographer can emphasize the focus point. A shallow depth of field can be achieved by increasing your aperture size.

Understanding Camera Lenses: Focal Length and Aperture

Basically, your first understanding of the focal length is simply how long the lens is. And in defying this common belief, Focal length is defined not as the measurement of the length of lens but the distance from the optical center of a lens attached to the camera body when the focus is of the lens is set to infinity. Focal length is measured in millimeters (mm).

Aperture is opening of a lens's diaphragm where light passes through. It is adjusted in f/stops and is generally expressed in numerical values such as 1.4, 1.8, 2, 2.8, 4, 5.6, 6.1, 8, 11, 16 and 32. Lower value f/stop has a wider aperture and provides more exposure, while higher f/stop values gives less exposure because of a smaller aperture.

To help remember this, the number value of the aperture is inversely proportional to the size of the aperture. High numerical value means smaller aperture and smaller numerical value means larger aperture.

Understanding White Balance

White balance is another assessment that good photographers check on their image. They need to ensure that colors are not affected by a light source. White is a manner of eliminating unrealistic color casts, so subject appearing white in person will be rendered as white in the created image. Proper setting of the white balance in the camera has to take into account the color temperature of a light source, which denotes to the warmth or coolness of the light.

Understanding Camera Autofocus

Camera Autofocus is another feature among digital camera nowadays. The camera sensor would intelligently adjust the camera lens to assume a good focus on the subject taken.

There two ways for the autofocus to work. The camera will use its contrast sensors to measure focus by assessing changes in the contrast. This is known as passive autofocus. The more contrast available on the subject, the more sharpness is assumed. Another way is by discharging a light signal to illuminate or estimate the distance to the subject. Once a focus is set by the autofocus sensor, it would set the lens to a new focusing distance. This process happens in a blink of an eye.

Factors affecting the autofocus are the light level, if the subject is in motion and amount of contrast of the subject. These factors are interdependent with each other. For example, you can able to achieve autofocus to a dim subject even though it has good contrast and this implies the proper selection of autofocus point.

Most cameras are equipped with an Autofocus beam. This is an active method of autofocus where visible light or infrared beam is emitted to help the autofocus sensors to detect the subject, especially if it is not adequately lit.

Autofocus is being used by new photographers to create sharp photographs if they do not have the knack yet in using manual focus.

Understanding How to Hold Your Camera

The proper way to hold and support your camera is by holding the body with your right hand and cradles the lens on your left palm with a proper grip on the lens barrel. Your left elbow should be propped on your torso to make your hold sturdy. Your foot should be half a pace ahead of the other to keep your upper body stable. This is the common hold and stance that most photographers use in most situations. Unless you will be using longer shutter speeds in your photography, it is required to use tripods to minimize camera shake at least to zero.

Qualities of Digital Photos

Good composition is what catches the eye of the viewer. It is the key element in planning how to plan to take the shot. The photographer should decide how to frame the subject, how far would you zoom or what would be the camera's position.

Proper focus and contrast can be a powerful quality of a good photograph. Subject with good details and contrasting colors can lead the viewer's eye to it.

If the viewer instantly understood why the photographer took the shot, it is a clear indication that the photograph is of high quality.

Understanding Bit Depth

Bit Depth measures how many distinct colors are available in an image color palette in terms of the number 0's and 1's, or known as "bits", which are used to specify each color. A single bit can store two values and in photography purposes, you can think of black and white. Two bits can store four values which can be black, white and two shades of gray and so on. Digital image have eight or sixteen bits for each of the three colors (red, blue and green) channels that define pixel values.

Every color in the digital image is created with the combination of the three primary colors: red, green and blue. As with any digital file, the building blocks of this file are bits. These bits are numbers zero (0) and one (1) and these numbers represent each color. The first level or a single bit would store two values. In photography, a single bit can store, for example, white and black. Next, if it would be a 2 bit file, there would be four values that it can store. Say, White and Black and at least two shades of gray. As the bit file increases, the number of values it stores increases exponentially. The more values it stores, the more shades of color would be present in the digital image file.

For a digital image to be created, it should start with at least eight (8) bits or to sixteen (16) bits level of each of the three primary colors (red, green, blue). These primary colors are referred as color channel. A pixel is created when the three primary colors are combined. Each primary color would be defined by bits per channel. The variation in this bit per channel would define the intensity of the primary color.

Understanding Sharpness

Sharpness means the clarity of detail in an image and can be an important creative tool for emphasizing texture. Proper technique can go a long way in improving the sharpness, but can be limited by your camera equipment.
There are factors that affect how you perceive sharpness. Image noise can be detrimental to an image but minimal amounts can help make the image look sharp. Camera shake can affect the sharpness and may cause blurs, so proper camera holding or proper shutter speeds can significantly improve the sharpness of the photograph.

Understanding Image Noise

Image Noise is a randomly-spaced bright pixel, specks, or lines which is more evident at higher ISO sensitivities, that is not present in the subject. This is a common nuisance of photographers in taking dark subjects or in low light condition. Image noise decreases the quality of the image and would cause a bit loss of detail. Grain in film photography is the equivalent of image noise in digital photography.

Understanding Dynamic Range

Dynamic Range is the difference between the brightest regions and darkest regions of an image. Dynamic range is measured in exposure value (EV). Exposure value is also known as stops.

HDR photography or High Dynamic Range photography is another way in creating stunning photographs. To simply discuss how it is done, the photographer would take three different photographs of the subject with different exposure, usually, one with lesser exposure, one with an adequate exposure and one who has higher exposure. After having images captured, the photograph would lodge the set of images in HDR software. This software will fuse these images to one image. There would be options available for the photographer to tweak the settings to obtain the photographer's taste on what the image would appear. You can try a free trial of software, and it offers presets and manual settings. There are number of HDR software available for download from the internet that you can try.

In order to have good images for HDR, the camera should be set on any sturdy surface, and of course, tripod is the best option. It is best that your subject should have no motion at all as you will be capturing multiple images. Any motion variation can be nuisance to an HDR photograph. For example, you are planning to take an image of a building, and by accident, there was a camera shake. The edges of building will not meet and blend properly then upon fusing them into one photo.

Higher end Digital SLRs have an exposure bracket function that would automatically create a minimum of three images with varying exposures. Unlike with entry level Digital SLRs, you have the manual adjust the settings to obtain varying exposures and this would take more time. The photographer should also ensure that settings are same on each image taken to make the quality of each image congruent. Post processing then would be easy then. Learning HDR is not an overnight skill but it would entail a bit of work and effort to perfect it. Once you get the grasp of it, be ready to amaze even yourself.

Chapter Two: Camera Equipment & Accessories

Camera Types & Accessories

In today's digital age, there are many camera types ubiquitously available in the current market. There are too many to mention in this guide and the list below represent only a partial list of those that are available during the writing of this guide. As you may know, cameras are one of the most rapidly changing markets in the industry. Upgrades and enhancements reflecting the technological development make new ones available and older ones obsolete.

Point and Shoot Cameras – these are ultra compact and light camera types. They function almost fully automatic and most brands have scene modes, where one can easily adjust the camera's settings on the situation. Lenses can have a decent zoom range but are not interchangeable.

Advanced Digital Cameras – this type plays between a point and shoot camera and a Digital SLR. Here you can use manual settings unlike the point and shoot camera.

Digital Single Lens Reflex - popularly known as the DLSR cameras, these are cameras are distinct because they give you the opportunity to change lenses as needed. Another notable difference is that these cameras are also more powerful than their smaller counterparts. It has a large sensor, more manual control and various automatic or point and shoot modes. These cameras allow one of the greatest flexibility to suit your photography needs and preferences.

Smartphone cameras- A relatively recent line of camera type is the prosumer camera. This is a combination of professional and consumer, which means these cameras are sold at consumer prices, meaning not too expensive to prevent the average consumer from purchasing them but still at professional level features. For example some models of Nikon belong to the prosumer line, allowing them to gain a significant share in the market. Their line of products is so successful that traditional professional level and expensive camera brands like Canon are following suit.

Camera accessories are another set of items that have a range of their own. Here is a list of some of some accessories every beginner and expert photographer may want in their gear:

Memory cards
Batteries
Card readers
Light filters-
Tripods
Monopods
Bags
Straps

Compact vs. Digital SLR Cameras

Compact cameras differ with Digital SLRs on its functionality. Compact Cameras almost runs in automatic mode which gives you limited adjustment options but offers the greatest ease in use. What it lacks in manual control is made up by its light weight and size. On the other hand a DLSR camera may offer better control but can be very bulky and heavy for your use.

Take note that there is no perfect camera. Instead of the camera dictating your photography style, it should be the other way around. Your style, preference and photography needs will determine which camera is best for you. For example if you are a beginner and you prefer to practice on your skills first before investing on more expensive models, then compact may be the best for you. If you want to go straight to a combination of beginner options mixed with advanced features and do not mind the weight and the price tag, then DLSR cameras are for you.

Selecting & Using a Camera Tripod

There are a number of different tripods in the market today, ranging from high end and low end brands, of course with variation on prices. These tripods also differ in material and the way they work. From the name itself, tripod is a photographic accessory with three telescoping legs and a head where the camera is attached. A tripod is used when sturdiness is required to take the shot. All tripods attached to the camera through a screw style lock.

The two common types of tripod head are the ball head and the pan-tilt head. The ball head type use a ball and socket to allow movement from a single point. You can control the angle of the head by just controlling the ball joint.
The pan-tilt head employs different controls and axes to pan and tilt the camera. There are two types of pan-tilt head. The 2 way head controls the panoramic rotation and the upward-downward tilt. The 3 way head controls the panoramic rotation, the upward-downward tilt and sideways tilt.

The telescoping legs have two common locking systems, the lever lock and the twist lock system. At the end of the telescoping legs are the feet. It is usually made of rubber for proper traction on the ground. There are other tripods feet that has spike for added grip to the ground and sturdiness.

Camera Flash, Part 1: Light Quality & Appearance

In situations that you need to properly illuminate your subject, that is the time that you would a source of light which is the flash. This source of light can come from the built-in flash on the camera or a flash unit called speed light.
You can control the intensity of the flash based on the lighting situation of the subject. You can also control the angle of the light source.

The difference of the quality of flash can pose a different effect on the subject. One factor is the creation of shadows. You have an entry level Digital SLR camera, and you will be using the built in pop flush to illuminate your subject. The pop up flash is directly pointing to your subject. The effect would be a strong light source that would a cast a strong shadow behind the subject and shadows within the subject that do not receive the light. This is the effect of a direct flash.

Another method is bouncing the light. This is a technique that would diffuse or soften the light and this would cast an almost minimal shadow. However, in bouncing the light, you have to consider the color of the area where you will bounce the light as this would create color cast on the subject. Also, you have to consider the surface or distance of the bouncing area.

Another way to illuminate your subject is using a reflector, but then again, reflectors do not discharge light on its own. It just bounces the light from the source to the subject.

Camera Flash, Part 2: Flash Ratios & Exposure

Flash ratios describe the ration between two figures, the amount of light that comes from the flash of your camera to the amount of light coming from natural light. Because the shutter speed does not affect light coming from your flash but it does affect natural light, then the flash ratio can be controlled. It is important to note that flash ratios do not have a limit but due to the intensity of natural light or the proximity of your subject, then varying flash ratios can be achieved.

0 flash ratios refer to a setting where there is no flash and only natural light is available. 1:8 to 1:2 is called the fill flash, this is also the setting that has the flash at its weakest and the exposure at its longest. On the 1:1 ratio, there is almost a perfect balance between the light produced by natural and flash sources. The flash is weak and the exposure is short. Finally, from 2:1 to 8:1, this represents the ratio that has the strongest flash but shortest exposure.

Camera Suggestions for Beginners, Intermediates & Advanced Photographers

There are many models and types of cameras, sometimes this range of options may cause you to become paralyzed preventing you from making a choice. Your clue to make the perfect choice lies on your personal preference or your familiarity with photography itself. If you are a beginner, then the smart phone camera or point and shoot cameras are your best choices. Brands like Samsung and Apple and their phones are the leaders in cameras on phones for beginners. For intermediate users, then advanced digital cameras may be the best for you. They allow you enough familiarity to use as with the point and shoot but also offer you the next level with its manual adjustments. For advanced photographers, your DLSRS are your best choice; these will offer you the best challenge with almost total control of taking one picture from another. Some of the most reputable brands in cameras are Panasonic, Nikon, Sony and Canon.

Chapter Three: Camera Lenses

Understanding Camera Lenses: Focal Length & Aperture

Focal length, usually expressed in millimeters (mm) is the label used to describe or name a lens. For example different kinds of lenses are a 24mm, a 35mm or other lens measurements. Note that the mm is not really a measurement of the length of the actual lens but refer to optical distance. The shorter the mm, your photo will have lowered magnification and wider field of view. The opposite is also true, the longer you mm, the better the magnification and the narrow the view. Aperture is the hole that found in the lens. It is the passage by which light enters and reaches the camera body for processing. If you adjust the diaphragm, you adjust the amount of light that enters in the aperture.

Using Wide Angle Lenses

These types of lenses are best used when you intend to highlight the size of the subject and highlight the depth of your photo. These are around 35mm lenses that provide more than 55 degrees field of view. If you intend to exaggerate the size of a nearby subject or shorten the size of a distance object, then these lenses are for you. Other applications for these lenses include subjects that involve interiors, landscapes and architecture.

Using Telephoto Lenses

Telephoto Lenses are being used in situations that you need to have a tight framing of your subject but you cannot be near to it. This is the time that you will need Telephoto Lenses or zoom lenses. Example of situations that a telephoto lens is required is when you are covering a sport event, wildlife and astrophotography.

A telephoto lens is designed to magnify a part of the subject and would appear as a full image. The magnification or zoom is controlled by twisting the lens barrel unlike with point and shoot cameras which the zoom is controlled by buttons. In greater magnifications, a tripod is required to have a sharper image of your subject because camera shake will be obvious, and capturing hand held could spell a missed opportunity.

Short telephoto lens ranges from a focal length of 85mm to 135mm. These can be used in hand-held shooting. It is best to use in portraiture or events such as wedding or baptism where you can be not that too close or to fully intrude the event.

Medium telephoto lens range between 135mm to 300mm and any focal lengths beyond 300mm are super telephoto lenses. Medium telephoto lenses are usually used in sports photography while Super Telephoto lenses are perfect for wildlife photography, wherein you do not want to disturb the normal situation.

Tilt/Shift Lenses: Using Shift Movements to Control Perspective

Shift lenses are used to solve challenges that involve depth of field and perspective limitations. Using tilt shift movement can give you the ability to adjust the place of the imaging circle of the lens in relation to the sensor of your digital camera. When you do this, you essentially change the center of perspective of the lens in relation to the center of perspective of the lens. When you tilt, the focus is no longer perpendicular to the line axis. For example, if you are trying to shoot a building in the middle, there is a tendency to focus on the center image alone and the periphery images will be lost. With shift movements, you can force the camera to focus on the middle while capturing the periphery too.

Tilt/Shift Lenses: Using Tilt Movements to Control Depth of Field

Another application of these lenses is the control of the depth of field. Most of your average cameras that are easily accessible in the market have very limited depth of fields. While some cameras have the feature of increasing the depth, it almost always comes at great cost in the image. It can cause camera images to be too soft because of diffraction. Images without tilt have the foreground clear but the background images a bit blurred and the background. To achieve optimum clarity, you may need to decrease your aperture. Knowing the manipulation of tilt will be beneficial when subject are either vertical or when taking portraits.

Take note that these shift lenses always pose a challenge even for experienced photographers. There is no set rule on achieving the image that you want. Instead, every occasion demands its own adjustments. To use tilt lenses, begin by putting your lens to zero title Assess your subjects, especially if they are two subjects on different areas. Focus your camera at the farthest from the subject and make your adjustments. When you have done it, begin tilting but tilt it slow, waiting for the perfect adjustment made evident by the clarity of all depths.

Macro Lenses: Magnification, Depth of Field & Effective F-Stop

Macro lenses are in the realm of macro photography. In this style, you are interested in capturing small image and then magnifying them into large size but still clear magnified versions, and then macro lenses are your tool of choice. It is important to note that depths of field for these lenses are extremely small because of the intent. The small aperture is the only way that such level of magnification is possible. To achieve the desired image, a combination of near perfect lighting, shutter speed that is slow and high ISO is needed. As the magnification increases, the f stop of the lens also increases with it. The f stop is a combination of depth of field which has increase and exposure times that are lengthened and diffraction risk is also increased.

Macro Extension Tubes & Close-up Lenses

These are your best add-ons to your camera if you want more magnification power. These tools can surpass the limit of your camera lens giving you a wider range of options in your subject. These tubes are cylinders that have a space in between to allow your lens to move even further from the sensor. When this is achieved, you gain more magnification. On other hand, close up lenses are directly attached in the front of your lens, similar to a lens filter. These lenses have the added effect of magnification without making your camera bulky as with an extension tube.

Lens Characteristics

There a variety of types of lenses, each having their own distinct characteristics. You will have the standard lens that is capable of taking images exactly as the naked human eye can do. There are also wide angle lenses that have shorter focal lengths but the trade off is that you gain a wider view angle. Telephoto lenses give you a narrow filed but can take images from a distance. While zoom lenses, allow you to make adjustments so that you can do both wide angle and telephoto lenses. Another type is the fisheye; this is used for wider fields that even a wide lens cannot achieve. Macro lenses are for the heavily magnified subjects while tilt shift lenses allow you to gain control over perspectives.

Camera Lens Flare: What It Is and How to Reduce It

If you take pictures under the sun or artificial light, you may notice that you capture lens flares or rays of light that are caught in camera. While it is generally an object that is unwanted in photos, there are times when it is kept for artistic purposes. These flares are unwanted especially when the rays become too large that they occupy a significant portion of the image. If you prefer not having lens flares in your image, then lens hoods are your choice. These devices, which are attached directly to your lens, can reduce these flares. Aside from the hoods, you can also purchase lenses with coatings that are already anti reflective and positioning your subject or objects around your subject so that flare is obstructed.

Camera Lens Quality: MTF, Resolution and Contrast

Lens quality is primarily derived from three aspects, modulation transfer function or MTF, resolution and contract. The MTF is a number that describes the level of brightness of your subject and how this brightness is retained as it goes through the lens. 1 is perfect or complete preservation of the light while 0 is the poorest. Resolution is the ability of the lens to capture details and contrast is the measure to differentiate lens with another. The more resolution your lens has the more detailed your picture will be. The more contrast you have, the finer your lines and edges in your picture will have.

Camera Lens Filters

A camera lens filter is a photographic accessory that can be attached to far end of the lens. There are different types of lens filter based on the material use and its function. Lens filters are used by photographers if they need to emphasize something on the image or an added technique to improve the composition technique. Other specialized filter lens would filter a specific ray light and would render very unusual colors.

In purchasing a lens filter, you must consider the size of your lens in mm and why would you use it. You just do not go around and attached a lens filter and shoot. Choose a right lens filter depending on a situation. Other lens filter like the UV filter also functions as barrier to avoid dust and smudges contaminating the lens itself.

Choosing a Camera Lens Filter: Polarizers, UV, ND & GND

Lens filter are important to achieve images that you want while removing any unwanted effects, like saturation, haze or glares. There are generally four types of filters, the polarizers, the ultraviolet or UV, the neutral density or ND and the graduated neutral density or GND. Each of these types has their corresponding uses and is best used when you have a specific subject matter in mind.

For example, your polarizers are meant to avoid glare and increase the levels of saturation. If you plan to take landscape and wildlife subjects, then this is the best filter for you. If you want subjects that are usually found in bright lights, such as mountains, rivers and waterfalls with the latter two having a tendency to reflect light, then your NDs are your choice because it can lengthen the time of exposure. The GND is best used for landscapes under dawn, dusk, rainy or any other lighting that is not considered neutral. UVs are all purpose filters.

Understanding & Using Polarizing Filters

Your polarizing filters are mainly for landscape photography. They work by limiting the light that passes through your lens and into the sensors. It will make colors more vivid, minimize glares from light sources outside your control and also decrease the contrast on sky and land. Because of the amount of light that is reduced by these filters, there is a danger of limiting too much light that the end result is a blurred image.

Using Graduated Neutral Density (GND) Filters

The pattern of light that is restricted by the GND filters make it best suited for landscape subjects. For example, if you are taking a picture of a landscape under the light of a progressing sun rise then the effect will be that of colors that are very vivid but simple, such as a progression of orange hues and dark colors. When you have to contend with these colors, then GNDs will be your choice.

Using Neutral Density (ND) Filters

By reducing light, these ND filters work best when you are also adjusting the exposure time, apertures and ISO for subjects that are in motion. Subjects that are best taken using these filters are moving waters. At the same time, if you prefer to show objects in motion by blurring, these filters are your choice.

Caring for Your Camera & Photos

A Camera is an investment and as with any other electronic device, they require proper care and handling. Each brand has specific instruction in handling and cleaning your camera and it is advised to follow it strictly. There are various ways to keep your camera cared for, such as avoiding moisture, proper handling and storage, avoiding bumps and other precautions. Never attempt to clean the interior and working mechanisms within the camera unless you are an expert.

Any speck of dust can wreak havoc on the sensitive lenses in the camera. Aside from taking care of the camera yourself, contact partner service centers of your camera's manufacturer for best results. Digital photos are best stored in multiple backups, aside from the memory card in your camera. For example, you can store them on external storages so they do not use up computer memory space. You can also save then on the virtual drives or on the cloud for added precaution against breakdown of physical drives.

Digital Camera Sensor Cleaning: Tools & Techniques

Sensor cleaning is the most sensitive procedure apart from fixing it. Since you are to get in touch with the most sensitive and expensive component of the camera, which is the sensor, this procedure entails a proper handling, equipment use and environment. For example, you are to clean a dirty sensor, so you have to be in an environment where there would be no dust or small particles that may lodge on the sensor.

How to Make Archival Digital Photo Backups

Preserving photos done in print require well known techniques such as framing, sealing and other techniques. While protection from the environment is the only thing that you need to contend to for physical photos, digital photos require an entire school of thought to preserve them. The rapid changes and developments in digital photography increase the risk of digital photos being either degraded or made unreadable with new technology.

Some considerations you need to make are the type of file of the photos and the storage device. For example, JPEG is the usual choice for storage because it offers smallest file size but the poorest in quality. On the opposite end is the DNG, it has the largest file size but has the best quality. JPEG is widely accepted and DNG is still being introduced. From hard disks to external storages to virtual devices, there is no one perfect storage device. Instead, choose redundant storage devices to best protect your digital photos.

How to Protect Online Photos: Copying, Watermarks & Copyrights

Every photo that you take is your intellectual property. You are due payment for its use, whether through royalties or outright purchases of the rights. When you share your photos online, it is not only made visible for the entire world to see but also made vulnerable to thefts and illegal reuse. There are various ways to do protect your online photo.

First is to make it difficult to copy. For example, you can create 2 layers out of the picture that you will post, one layer is the actual image and the other is a transparent layer in the top. This way when someone attempts to right click and save your image, they will be saving the transparent image not the real one. You can also show the picture as part of a slideshow. The simplest method is to disable the right click function on your website entirely.

Another way is to put watermarks in the picture itself. This can be easily done with photo editing software. You can either put an entire watermark over the picture; put a frame around the picture with your name on the frame and other means to permanently embed your name on the photo.

Finally, you need to put in a copyright. Most websites automatically add a copyright every time you upload a picture and under the law of some countries, like the US and the UK, a photo made available is already protected under copyright laws. Alternatively, you can also edit the properties of your raw files so that it automatically adds a copyright notice on the file property itself.

While there is no guarantee that using any of the above techniques will guarantee a 100% protection level for your photos, every bit of step must be taken to at least delay or discourage would be thieves of your hard work.

Chapter Four: Photography Techniques

Using Your Camera

To efficiently use your camera, one should know and understand each and every button and functionality of its camera model. First thing is to read the manual. A lot of excited new camera owners would go out and test the camera without fully reading the manual. The manual would give you the understanding of the brains on how your camera works, how to take care of it, how to clean to it and how to store it.

Using Camera Shutter Speed Creatively

Playing with your shutter speed would create different effects in your photographs. Either you want to freeze motion or show motion, shutter speed setting is the key on achieving these different effects. For example, you can freeze a specific scene without any blurring. To do this, you need to boost your ISO to a high level such as setting your aperture to around f/2.8 to 4.5. This will hasten the shutter time that can increase the chance of your camera in getting a specific second in the scene. On the other hand, you can even create blur to depict motion in your images. To do set your aperture to 5.6. Choose conditions with low light and then move the camera as needed.

Reducing Camera Shake with Hand-Held Photos

If you are capturing hand held, sturdiness is the key to get that image sharp. You have to hold your camera properly and have the right settings to avoid any blurs. This means that tripods are indispensable in this attempt. Set your camera on these tools to reduce any camera shake. However, there will be times when you do not have access to a tripod and in these cases; you need to rely solely on your hands to stabilize the camera.

Some techniques that you can use involve using your own body to stabilize the camera. This can be done by planting yourself firmly in the ground through sitting, kneeling or propping yourself against a wall. Use anything solid, such as a table or any surface to push your camera against or your hands and elbows to keep yourself and your camera as stable as possible. Hold your camera with both hands relaxed, one hand under the lens and the other on the body of your camera.

Digital Exposure Techniques: Expose to the Right, Clipping & Noise
Subjects

Digital exposure refers to the three aspects of a camera that are manually adjusted to create the perfect balance. These are the shutter speed, the aperture and the ISO. To create the best exposure, you need to make real time adjustments to these three elements, often one adjustment very different from another. When you make these changes, your images attain the best possible clarity. There are three techniques to achieve this exposure level.

First is the expose to the right, this is an attempt to move the histogram to the right so that it the image will be over exposure. This gives your image enough brightness to clarify the details and avoid unwanted shadows. The danger with too much exposure is called clipping. This happens when a portion of the image is so bright or over exposed the details are lost. Clipping is usually avoided when using even auto shots but when there is too much brightness, especially in landscape photography, the image clips on bright areas. You need to adjust your exposure compensation to make up for the clipping.

Finally, another concept in photography is called noise. These are grains or specks that become visible in your photo, which reduces the overall clarity of your image. It is similar to old printed photographs, which is why other photographers purposely create noise to recreate the effect. Noise appears due to different settings in your camera. The pattern of the noise will give you a clue on how it was formed. For example, when you have too fast of an ISO, it will result to a random pattern. Colored specks or fixed pattern is due to long exposure. Noises that are banded are due to shadows.

Photography in Fog, Mist or Haze

Fog, Mist or Haze are natural occurrences that do not happen most of the time. These are situations that the photographer should be ready anytime or at least anticipate for it to happen. Since these weather-related situations do not happen all year round. Shooting while there is a fog has a great impact on your photograph. It evokes a different feel and emotion. A proper camera setting should properly capture the fog or mist, without losing the detail of your subject or depending on your composition technique. These weather elements can be overcome using a variety of techniques. You can add more exposure compensation or longer exposure time.

However, instead of being overcome, these elements are actually preferred by photographers because of its effect on the images. To make the most out of these elements and to increase the dramatic effect of the image, you can highlight shapes, depth and light. For example, you can take an image of the rays of light piercing through the fog by choosing a correct location where to shoot.

Introduction to Macro Photography

In macro photography, you may need specialized lenses for this genre. For starters, you can initially start with your kit lens. Macro shots would make tiny subjects look large. Best subjects are tiny insects and small intricate parts of the flowers. Macro lenses are quite expensive compare to kit lenses. For advanced photographers, they are calculating the scale on how they can double the subject or the image size.

For those who cannot afford to purchase a separate macro lenses, there are other techniques to achieve macro shots. Take the fool zoom which is 55mm. For example, the subject would be an ant. You can use manual focus and took the shot of the ant and in raw file. Normally, it would appear small in the photographer. In post-processing, you can crop the photo, tweaked the contrasts and sharpness and then have a simple macro shot.

Next is by using a 50mm 1.8 prime lens. You need a fully opened the aperture to 1.8. Now, still using the same kit lens above put your camera on full zoom at 55mm. You can align your lenses together. With the prime lens, the ones with the CPU contacts are faced to the side of the subject. You need to find the right interval between the lenses to obtain microscopic effect of the prime lens. A really steady hand is required if you are not able to design a crude barrel that would hold the lenses together. Start practicing with stationary subjects and progress to moving subjects. With the two above methods, it would be a challenge to mirror the quality if subjects are taken from an actual macro lens.

Intro & Common Obstacles in Night Photography

Night photography is another challenge for the photographer. How would you have a stunning image out of a dark subject? The only source of illumination would be the reflected light from the moon and from other light sources like streetlamps or collective city lights.

Your subjects are not always properly illuminated. It takes another set of photographic techniques to capture the night scene and have a stunning image.
There are factors that you need to consider in taking night photographs. First is the lighting situation of your subject, the size of the subject and how you would compose. The key is how to not to make your night shots do not look dark. Now is the time to play around with what you learned on the triangle of exposure.

Making the Most of Natural Light in Photography

One of a great skill of photography is how he sees light and how the light will affect his photographs. Often, light is the single most important factor has the greatest effect on the quality of your image. If you are a landscape, nature or outdoor photographer, natural lights can be your greatest ally or enemy. There are three components in natural light that you can work with to suit your preference, these are the weather, the time and then the direction of your camera.

Anything that is between the sun and your subject is considered in photography as the weather. This means that clouds, fog, mist, haze, rains and other elements have an effect on the quality of light that illuminates your subject. Knowing how one type of weather affects your image in one manner compared to another type can be used to your advantage. For example, storms can cause high contrast, while sunsets make the land area darker.

For time of the day, the location of the sun can also be taken into consideration. For example, expect the highest contrast during the mid day when the sun is at its almost vertical position to your subject. Colors will be very bright with varying hues of redness during the sunrise and sunset and expect pastel colors during dawn, dusk and the twilight. Adjusting your camera setting based on these potential effects on your image for your preferred results.

Portrait Lighting with One Light: Introduction

Portrait photography is a field that has one of the highest potential to convey human emotions, feelings and features. These are often done with the subject's face in close up in a controlled environment such as a studio or indoors. These venues give greater control to the photographer in composing the image. One of the most important considerations in portrait photography as with other types is lighting. The most basic but still challenging portrait shots are those done with only one source of lighting.

Your main source of light is either call the key or main light. Other lighting is only used to further enhance the image. You need to know how large the light is focused and how it is directed. Take time to play around with these two controls, each combination will produce its own set of lighting effects. For example, if you have large light, you will have soft light, which is able to reduce imperfections. If you have a smaller light, then you will have hard light, which makes finer lines, wrinkles, freckles and other details more apparent. If you shine the line directly in front of the subject, the entire face will be illuminated. Focus it on the left and the right side will be darker. Shine it above, and then the shadow will be on the lower side of the face.

Portrait Lighting with Two Lights: Fill Light

On top of your key light, you can have additional light sources, which are called fill light. These lights further reduce the presence of shadows, its depth and can remove the hard edges in portraits. Use the same principles as with the main light, such as size and direction of the light. Another consideration is how the fill light can "fill in" gaps made by the key light. For example, if your light source comes from the right and you have no way of moving it, then you can position your fill light on the left.

Specialty Portrait Lights: Background, kickers, hair, rim, etc.

Aside from your key and fill lights, there are other options for you to add more light into your image.

The background light illuminates the backdrop on the subject creating an aura like sheen around the head of the subject. This is mainly done so that the subject is seen to be distinct from the background. The kicker is a light is placed directly above or to the sides of the subject. This is used when you want to highlight the sides and the shoulders of the subject. The hair light is used to highlight the hair or to make the head distinct from the background, when the head has a tendency to blend with the background. The rim light is used to create a halo effect around the entire head.

Studio Portrait Lighting Styles & Diagrams

If you intend to use more than one light source, then you can be guided by different lighting styles, each with their own diagram. There are 5 lighting styles that can be used for basic portrait set up. These are the paramount, the Rembrandt, the loop, the rim and the split. Paramount is meant to be highlighting the cheekbones and make the skin look clearer. The Rembrandt is meant for more dramatic effects such as creating shadows in the cheek area. If your subject has an oval face, the loop lighting style is best. If you want to position your subject with his head looking sideways, then the rim lighting is appropriate. Finally, split lighting is used to create the illusion of having leaner features. Refer to this link for the appropriate placing of your light sources.

Chapter Five: Composition

Composition

Properly composing your photographs is the fundamental technique to have a quality and exquisite images. Your photograph should catch the eye of the viewer and the photography itself would tell or express the story or emotion without the photographer needing to explain it. It is a skill. It could be learned or it could be inherent with the photographer. Most photographers agree that instead of focusing on the technical side of the art, beginners should start with composition. Similar to painting, it is not always the chemical makeup of the paint but the way the painter draws and brushes are the things that can make or break the final product. In composition, try to be as simple as you can, this way your viewers will be able to understand the message that you are trying to convey. Focus on one subject and then remove any clutter.

Try to fill the entire frame with an image, while blank spaces are also used for artistic effect, too much empty space will only create confusion and a sense of something lacking in the viewers. Experiment also with ratios, try vertical shots as much as horizontal ones. Adjust as needed so you learn at the same time. Another way to compose is to avoid the center. Traditionally, you can put your subject directly in the center of the frame but for added effect, you can move the subject away from the middle and your viewers will see the same picture but this time convey another message.

Try to capture lines that lead your viewers' eyes towards a specific direction. This way you can focus their vision towards your message. An alternative to leading lines is the use of diagonal lines, both of these can remove the static feeling on photos. Pay as much attention to the background, this can both resolve blank spaces and add message.

The Rule of Thirds

Rule of thirds is a composition technique in taking photographs. In this technique, you will be dividing the frame in three spaces vertically and horizontally. Instead of centering the subject in relation to its background, placing the subject within two vertical lines is said to produce more interest and add impact on your photo. This rule allows the subject to flow seamlessly with the rest of frame and on each section. By applying the rule, it prevents a subject to cutting the frame into half or smaller sections instead of cohesive whole.

For example if you take a photo of a lone tree in a landscape, if you put the tree right on the center, then you create a left and right space that is blank and a top and bottom landscape which does not have the subject on it. However, if you situate the tree somewhere along the lines where they intersect, it removes the partitioned effect.

Using Diagonals for Dynamic Photos

Pushing the boundaries in photography is an everyday occurrence. While straight vertical and horizontal lines were once the norm, this rule is being challenged by the use of diagonals. A lot of photographers are bending this rule to add pizzazz on their photos. The advantage in taking these diagonal lines is that it keeps the viewers on their toes and allows them to become more curious of the picture. Through these lines, you direct the gaze of your viewers towards the message that you want to transmit. This also gives motion or a sense of movement to an otherwise static image.

Negative Space - Sometimes Less is More

Most photographers try to lessen the negative space since the rule is to try to fill up the frame as much as possible. However, the trend in photography is purposely to have negative space. This is meant to create and attract attention so that your viewers will be able to follow the message that you intend to relay. This also provides additional emphasis to the subject or the focus of your image.

Image Stacking & Multiple Exposures

Image stacking refers to the technique used to remove the sacrifices that most photographers have to make to maintain sharpness, depth of field and other characteristics in one picture. The technique involves taking multiple exposures while adjusting your camera to gain the best image quality on one aspect at the expense of another. Then another set of exposures are taken and the camera is adjusted so that the sacrificed other area is boosted again. From these multiple shots, stacking is done to combine both strong parts and covering up the weaker areas of the photo.

Using the High Dynamic Range (HDR) Feature in Photoshop

In Adobe Photoshop, you can change your photo so that it becomes an HDR. In this technique, you can choose from a set of exposures and then combine them into a single file. To do this, go to Photoshop and then use the HDR tool. This is found on file, then automate then merge to HDR. Choose the set of photos that you want to merge. You can also choose to align source images if you have taken pictures without a tripod.

Once done, you will have a file that has the combined histogram of all the separate images. Take note attempting to this will use up significant computing load for your computer. When this is complete, you need to convert the resulting file to an image, around 16 to 8 bits so you can see the preferred result.

Extending Depth of Field Using Focus Stacking

Focus stacking is a technique used to gain as much depth of field as possible. This is often the technique of choice when you are taking photos that are macro, low light or landscape. Image stacking will allow you to gain more depth of field even when you have your main subject magnified. It will also increase brightness without necessarily affecting exposure time. When you are taking landscape shots but the increased depth of field suffers from softness, then image stacking is also the technique that you can use to solve this issue.

To do this technique, you need to take multiple exposures of your subject. As you progress in exposures, you increase the focusing distance. Once you have this set of exposures, you will then stack on image to another, and each pixel is then aligned to each pair until you get the desired quality. Once done, you can process it to a photo editing software, such as Photoshop to combine all the exposures into one clear file.

F-Stop Stacking: Depth of Field & Corner Sharpness

Despite the stacking techniques, there are still occasion when softness is still found on your image. To counter this and still achieve sharpness, then f-stop stacking is needed. To do this, you need to take photos of the same subject over and over again but this time altering the f stops on every succeeding picture. This way, you can still extend the depth of field to your desired level but still keep the sharpness because of the stacked images.

Corner sharpness is often sacrificed in areas farthest from the center of the lens. Due to different lens manufacturing techniques, there are varying degrees on the blurring of the corners. To achieve the sharpness that you want on the corners, you need to use higher levels of f stop. However, the higher your f stop is the clearer your corners become but the center will be blurred. Again, this can be resolved by f-stop stacking.

Chapter Six: Special Topics

The Perfect Selfie

Photography is not always serious and artistic; sometimes even photographers indulge themselves in fun, relaxed and even casual ways to take a photo. The infamous selfie has made its way to popular culture and with the camera market offering almost everything you need to take a selfie; you have no excuse not to make yours the perfect one.

Taking the perfect self involves a combination of photography skills, the right equipment and of course creativity. It is important to consider the source and intensity of the lighting. The sun is best source of light for both photos and the selfie. It has the right brightness to flatter your face without causing unnecessary shadows or dark spots. While the sun or other light sources are ideal, without the proper place, you will not be able to maximize its fullest benefit.

Whether you use the sun or an artificial source of light, position yourself or the light source if possible in front of you and within your eye level. This ideal location has several effects to your face. First it can brighten your face making it livelier and younger. Next, it will soften the edges of your jaw, nose and other facial or body parts. In the wrong place and despite your best efforts, the light can make you look darker, aged and tired. In the right place and sometimes even without any effort, the light can enhance your features.

Also, be very careful on the settings you use on your camera. For example, the camera flash is definitely discouraged. Any flat surface in your face, such as your forehead or cheeks will have a light glare effect. Your eyes may also reflect the flash causing the redeye effect. Blemishes, scars and other imperfections that you may prefer to hide will be made crystal clear when you use the flash during the selfie. For best results, turn off the automatic flash before you take a selfie.

If you are using smart phones that come equipped with two cameras, one on front and the other on the back, use the back camera to take the selfie. While this may seem counterintuitive, the front camera usually produces lower resolution pictures compared to the back.

Also, tilt your face at angle; this will remove the perception of flatness in your face and show depth and lines that will enhance your look. Other tricks that you can do are to take a selfie while in front of a fan to allow your hair to move and produce an outdoor or windy effect. Whether you use a digital or a phone camera, always take a picture with the camera above your head. When it is below, your face will look larger and rounder. While taking the photo from above will make your face look tighter and more angular.

A very popular tool that has taken the selfie culture by storm is the monopod. This is essentially a stick that can be comfortably grabbed by a hand and has enough length to allow camera to take a wide angle picture. The feature that makes the monopod interesting is that it most comes with a wifi or Bluetooth remote control that can allows you to click the camera to take the photo while still holding the monopod on your outstretched arm.

Every little bit of creativity counts when taking your selfie, whether it is wearing a bright red lipstick to attract attention to your lips, making funny faces to make the selfie more interesting or capturing a background with you, a perfect selfie is never out of reach.

Capturing Nature and Landscape Scenes

One of the most rewarding but at the same time challenging photography subject is nature or landscape shots. Taking these shots well is often a mark of photographer that has progressed from being a beginner shooting only in environments with their full control to an intermediate, on their way to expertise. The reason behind the challenge of these kinds of shots is the lack of control you have on the environment. While you can definitely choose the place and time of taking the photo, you will soon realize that you will gradually lose control. The sun will soon set, robbing you of your natural light, subjects such as wildlife cannot be made to stay on their pose and objects are relatively unmovable. You have to rely primarily on your photography skills and equipment to capture Mother Nature it all its untamed beauty.

The most important consideration you need to make is to tap the limit of your depth of field. This will allow you to take as wide as an expanse as possible when you take the photo. Instead of a limited area, with depth of field, you can capture as much of the landscape as possible. This will give you a combination of focus on the closest image in your camera and depth on the farthest image. Increase the depth of field by adjusting your aperture setting to the lowest.

Take note, this is often a balancing act. The lower your aperture is the less light enters the camera. When there is less light, there is a tendency for your photo to be either dark or blurred. Compensate by adjusting your ISO or shutter speed to cope with the aperture setting. The effect of this setting is that any minor motion will cause significant blurring. A tripod will keep your camera stable and do wonders to keep the settings you want intact but at the same time avoid the blurring.

Most beginners fail to capture the sky as part of the landscape shot. They are so focused on the terrain that the blue, clouds and other wonders of the sky are forgotten. If the sky is blank on your shot, it is best to devote only a small portion of the photo for the sky. However, if you have a sky that is caught in either dusk or dawn, or with dark looming clouds or light feathery ones, make the most out of the offering of nature to you.

Aside from taking wide angled shots, you may also consider taking photos of landscapes that provide varying levels of perceptions, such as fore and backgrounds. These perceptual illusions give your photo added sophistication. A perfect example is taking a picture of a rock formation in the foreground, with a patch of trees behind, a herd of animals farther and a massive mountain the background. This will help viewers pass through each of the grounds.

Despite the vastness of the landscape, you also need to choose a subject that will be the main focus of the entire photo. For example, if you are taking a photo of a field of flowers, instead of taking the picture of the entire field, pick a flower and then use the remaining field as a backdrop. This will give your viewers something to latch on even in a large image provided by the landscape.

It is a misconception that the best time to take a landscape photo is during the day, particularly in calm and relaxed environments. While a sunny day can be the best landscape for a beginner, a true photographer will take on the challenge of taking photos on all kinds of weather. When you are confident on your skills, consider pursuing other kinds of weather to improve your skills even further. For example, tall grass taken on a windy day can give you a shot that is both landscape and movement. A sky carrying dark rain clouds will give a more somber feeling in your photo. Most photographers on the other hand refer to dawn and dusk as being the golden hours in photography. This is the time that landscapes are at their best when lighted by the perfect light of the sun during these specific times.

Of course, nature is not only about stationary landscapes and terrain. One of the better subjects in nature photography is capturing nature as it moves. Whether it is a drop of dew in the life at the break of dawn, the violent waves that crash into a seawall or even the rare bolt of lightning caught on camera, nature photography can also be about movement. There are two challenges here, first is the technical one. For capturing objects in motion, you must adjust your shutter speed to make the speed longer. The second and important challenge is patience. The perfect time to catch movement cannot be predicted. Sometime the scene will already present itself within a few seconds when you are ready. There are also times when you will have to wait until the perfection conditions are in place.

One of the best settings that you can take a photo is the elusive water mirror. This is the time when a natural formation, such as a mountain, trees, animals or any other landscape is mirrored by a calm and perfectly positioned body of water, such as a pond or a lake. This is best taken during the golden hours. Use slow shutter speeds and adjust the aperture as needed until you take the desired effect.

While the photography may only be about nature, it does not mean that you need to exclude other persons in the photography. Having human subjects in the midst of rolling hills or another subject emerging from a rippling lake can add an entirely new dimension in your nature photography.

Finally, taking out of the box and rarely used points of view can add another level of interest in your work. Instead of the usual spots you use to take photos, you may consider another area. For example, taking on a picture of field can be taken on top of a tree and partially obstructed by tree branches and leaves. You can also position your camera so that it is on the level of the ground giving the illusion that the photo was taken in the perspective of the wildlife.

For camera accessories on this kind of photography, you may bring lens hoods; polarizing filters, tripod, neutral density filters and other similar equipment will be needed. Apply the same principles in photography, such as the rule of thirds, proper lighting and source of the light and other guides. Remember to balance between your aperture, ISO and shutter speed until you achieve the desired effect in your photo. For more detailed camera settings that can match your desired landscape preference, you can visit this link.

Why Not To Depend Solely On Software Edits

As powerful as software that can edit photos to your preference, these tools have their own limits. The amounts of manipulation this software can provide are extremely dependent on the raw photo that you have taken. For example despite its features, the more you boost the brightness, sharpness or other characteristics of a photo, the more unnatural the photo becomes.

Also, there is a drawback on using the software itself. This software is expensive and most features can only be used after lengthy training. The tools within the software are not easily learned overnight and even experienced users only have scratched the tip of the software's potential. Also, if you ever have the money to purchase and the time and patience to learn it, you will also need a computer that can handle the changes that you make. While an average computer can run the software, only the most basic of changes can be used without computer lag. For more intensive editing, you need a more powerful computer.

There is an ongoing debate on the use of software that can edit raw photographs. Much of the dilemma revolves around the ethical issues surrounding the photos and how it misrepresents the subject in the photo. The manipulation of photos defeats the age old tradition that pictures can never tell a lie. The moment a camera takes a picture, it is an accurate and 100% correct depiction of an actual subject or event. However with manipulation through software edits, not only can realistic fakes be introduced but also these edits are added together along with the real photos. As a result, viewers of the photo are either desensitized or unable to discern with edited or raw pictures or no longer trust the art of photography.

No other place in society is edited photos more argued than in media. When newsrooms, print and other broadcast media are reaching millions of audience and viewers and they present them with altered pictures, it is essentially propagating a lie. This results to a false sense of reality that has both short and long term consequences. Another issue is that these media companies are not completely transparent on their policies on edited pictures.

However, aside from media, other industries and genres are also participating in the debate. For example, wildlife photography is considered to be exactly as the name implies, a photo of the wild in its most natural and honest state. However, with software editing the very purpose of wildlife photography is defeated producing a fake version of the real deal. Notable wildlife photographers have been called out on this editing, one them even published a book with more than one-third of the photos were considered as altered.

Turning Your Photos into Masterpieces Using Photoshop and Instagram

Take your art to the next level by turning your photos into masterpieces using Photoshop and Instagram. While some purists may resist the temptation of using these software and social media platforms, no one can deny the ease and popularity of these tools. Even the beginner photographer can instantly lift his photo to something great with just a few clicks of the mouse or the taps of a finger.

Photoshop or other photo editing software is capable of high level photo revisions and editing. This software has almost a limitless combination of tools and features that you can use to turn a drab photo into something bright and interesting. While Photoshop is mostly used by professionals, even beginners can make use of its most basic of features and then learn as they use the software.

Some of the basic features that you use to alter or even correct some errors in your photo are changes in color selection, adjustments in the brightness, reduction of noise and removal of red eyes. These can be done with just one click of a button. This is made possible by automatic tools that are pre programmed into correcting the most common mistakes made by photographers on a raw photo. In just one click, you can remove the glare caused by your camera flash in your eyes. You can instantly make a picture brighter when you have taken the picture without enough natural light.

There are other features of Photoshop that you can use for your specific needs. It can compress the size of the picture, which gives you more options when importing or exporting to other uses. You can change the colors, brightness, sharpness and other characteristics of not only the entire photo but also specific areas in the photo, while keeping the rest raw. You can select sections of the picture, remove with the rest or merge with another photo. You can rotate, crop, layer and make other changes.

For glamour purposes, Photoshop can be indispensable. You can remove unwanted imperfections or blemishes. Wrinkles can be flattened, scars can be erased, dark skin can be lightened, and pale skin can be tanned and other skin changes. Even the entire body shape can be changed, from being round to becoming lean. The potential of the software is virtually limited only by your expertise on its use and your creativity. Instagram is another user friendly mobile app that can automatically use filters for the desired effect.

Things Remember When Taking Photos & Avoiding Common Mistakes

Do's

Plan ahead. While photography can be a spur of the moment activity, you can benefit greatly with careful planning. For example, if you want to take landscape shots, then you need to check on the shooting conditions. What time is best? What is the weather like? Will you have access to plugs to charge? Do you have enough memory cards? Will you need filters, lens hoods, tripods or other accessories?

Make full use of the LCD. This will give you almost a complete view of the image that will be taken when you press shoot on the camera. This is invaluable because it will help you make the adjustments as needed. Aside from the actual LCD, this usually comes with a grid to help you follow the rule of thirds, measure exposure and other adjustments that you can do before clicking. Also most cameras have LCD that can help you see towards your subject even with low light.

Take care of your tools. Modern cameras today are built to be sturdy and often stand the test of time and their rigorous use. However, even these cameras will fail when they are not maintained properly. For example, it is a common mistake to touch the lens of the camera and then wiped haphazardly with any cloth.

Find your style and niche. There are hundreds or perhaps even thousands of photography styles out there, some very similar, some distinct, some trendy and some classics. As a beginner, you may want to try everything at once. However, it is highly recommended that you put your focus one or few styles. Choose the style that is most appropriate for you, most accessible and most important feel most passionate about. Then become an expert at it and then move to another until you develop your personal style.

Make mistakes. This may seem counterintuitive but making mistakes is actually something preferred in photography. There is no such thing as perfection but you can learn from the mistakes you make. Use these errors are stepping stones towards enhancing your craft. When you have these real life errors, you will challenge yourself in coming up with real life solutions.

Don'ts

Use auto. While the automatic setting can be truly heaven sent because of the relative ease it allows you in taking pictures, this setting often robs you of the opportunity to enhance your photography skills. Get out of your comfort zone or in this case, the point and shoot setting. Experiment with your adjustments as often as you can. Remember, even the auto shots have their limitations. For example, extreme light conditions cannot be addressed properly by the auto setting and you will eventually have to do manual adjustments.

Be a lone wolf. Photography is best learned and developed in the company of likeminded individuals. When you surround yourself with other photographers, you can learn from those that came before you. Learn from the latest techniques or attend classes with them. Visit galleries and exhibitions of their work and take inspirations from them. While you can certainly study on your own, you will open yourself to a wider learner experience with them. Crawl through social media. Follow photographers in Instagram, follow the Tweets, and subscribe to Pinterest and other social media that host photographers and their works. This way you can also get inspiration even through your computer or smart phone.

Ignore photography ethics. Despite your best intentions, you may find yourself being confronted by cultural or ethical issues related to taking photos. This is especially the case when you are traveling to foreign land without the benefit of understanding their culture. Since photos are one of the must do's when traveling, being mindful of the proper photography conduct is important. Even within your country, there are some places where photos are not only discouraged but also considered illegal. For example, some cultures ban people from taking pictures of their religious artifacts, while some do not mind you shooting your camera inside churches. Almost all military installations disallow you from taking pictures, especially of their buildings and vehicles.

Be technology dependent. The best and most expensive camera and accessories will still up the worst photo without one key ingredient, your creativity. Do not rely solely on your tools and its adjustments. Learn to use your gut feeling and follow your instinct when taking photos. Sometimes, breaking photography rules will give you the opportunity to discover a new style that you can call your own. While the technical aspects of photography are not something to ignore, you need to put your focus on compositional aspects, which technical aspects will support.

Samples

Rule of Thirds

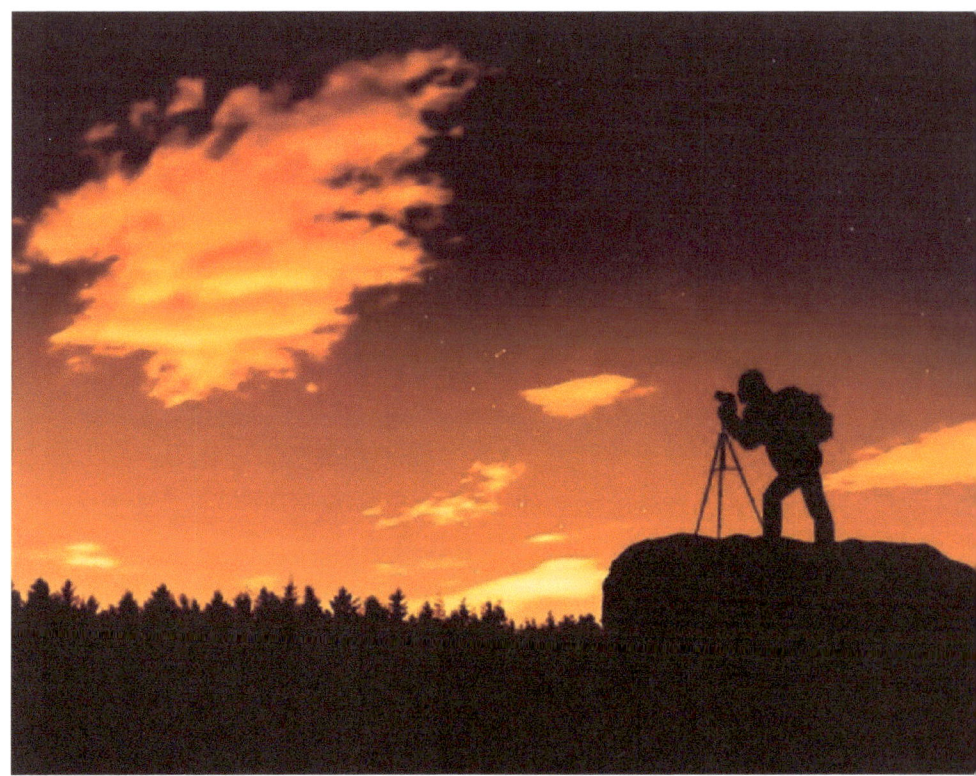

Landscape

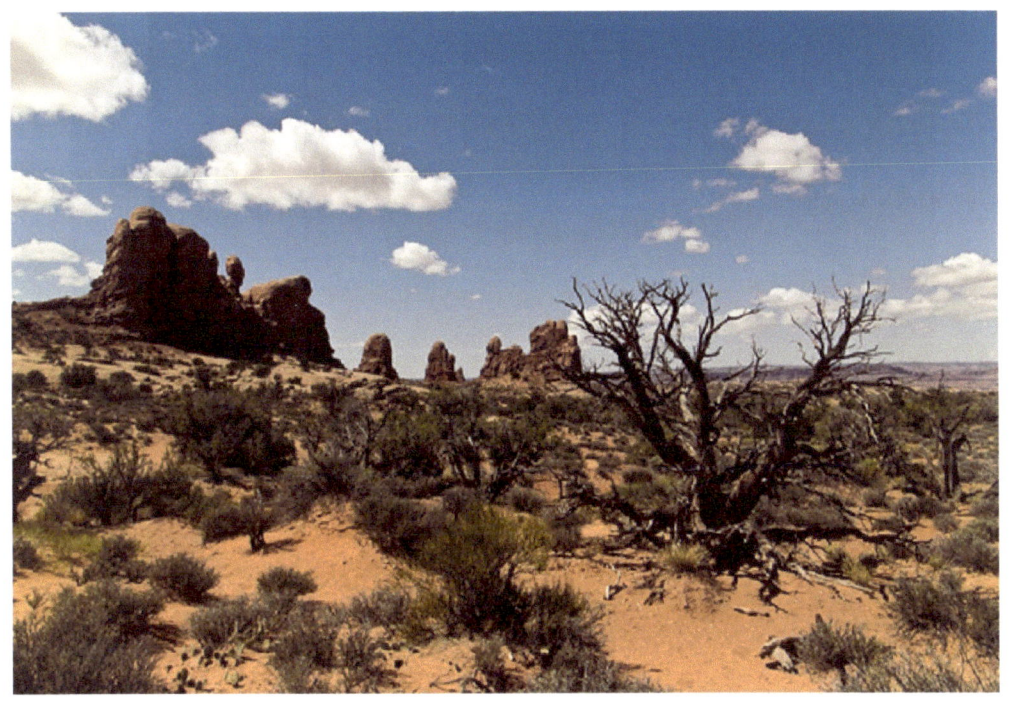

Diagonal

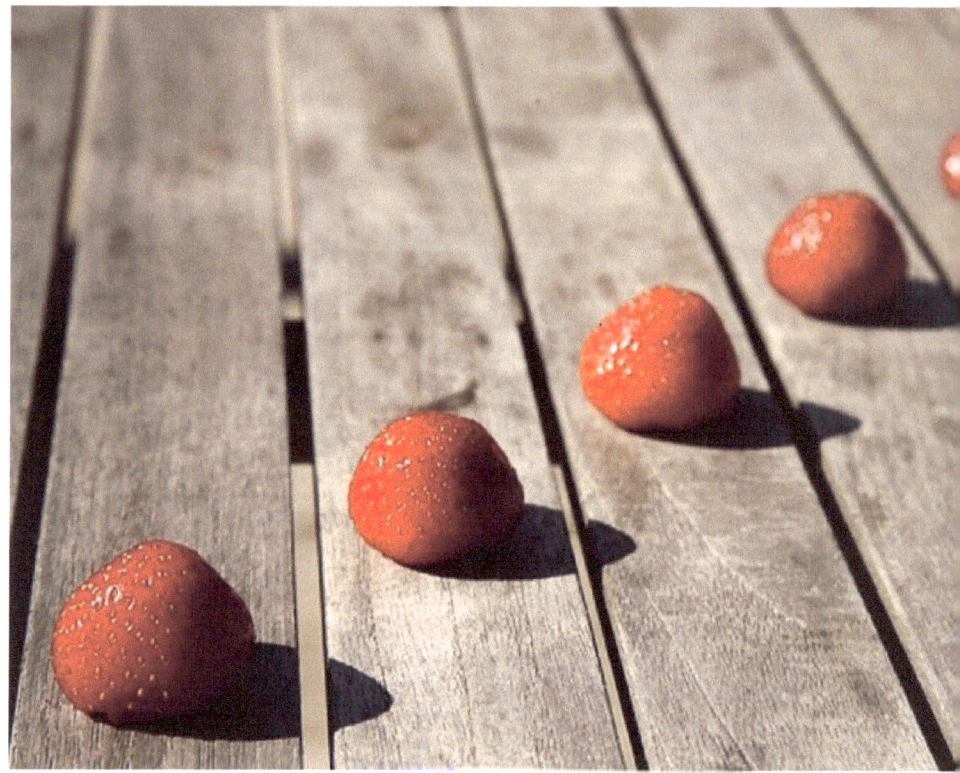

Fog

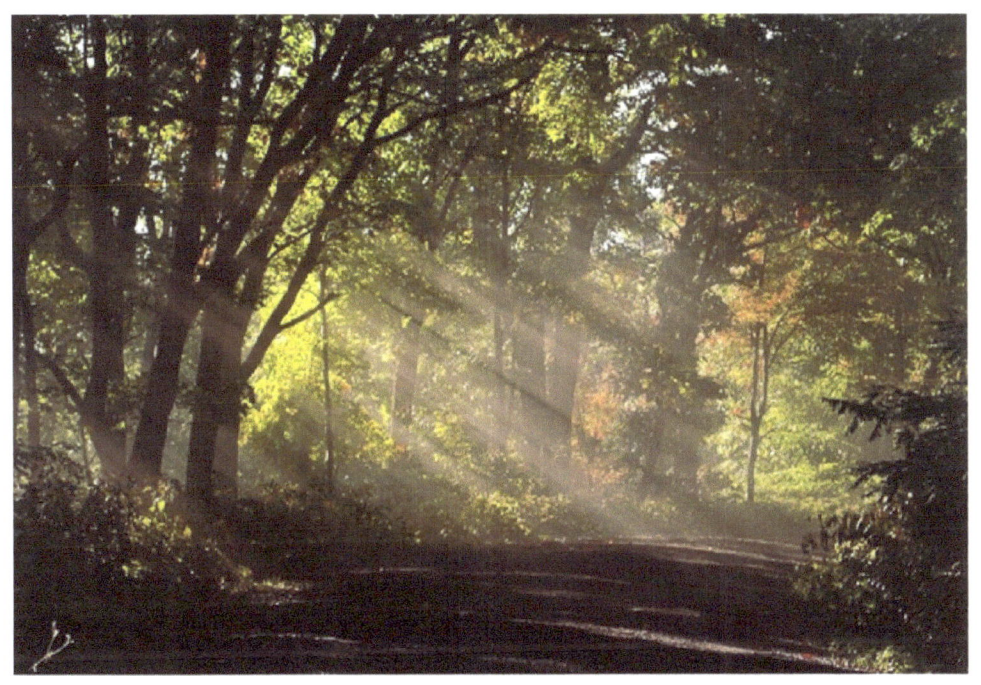

Macro

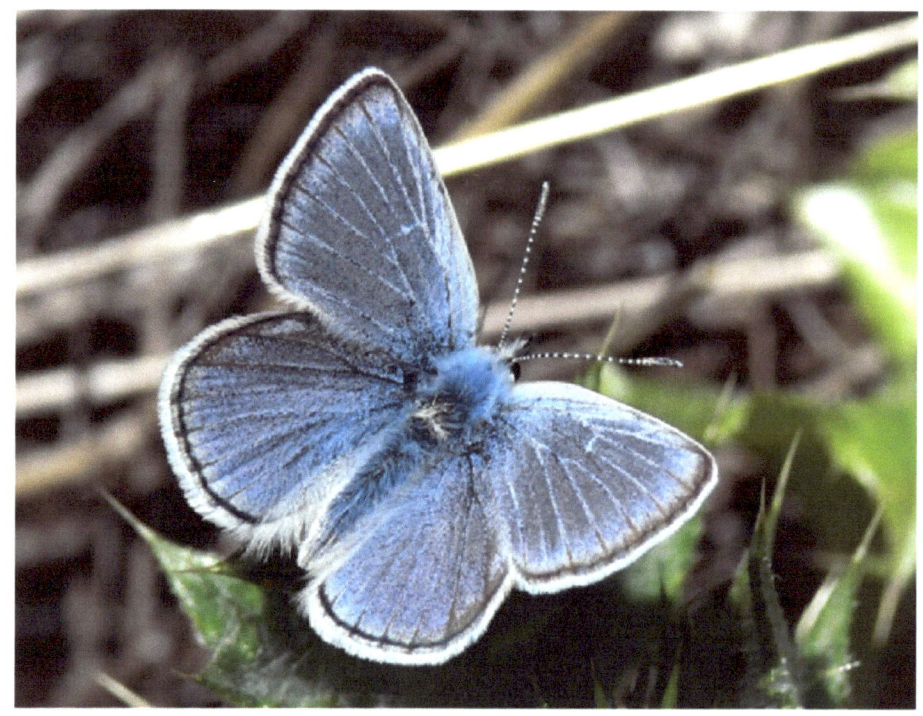

Portrait

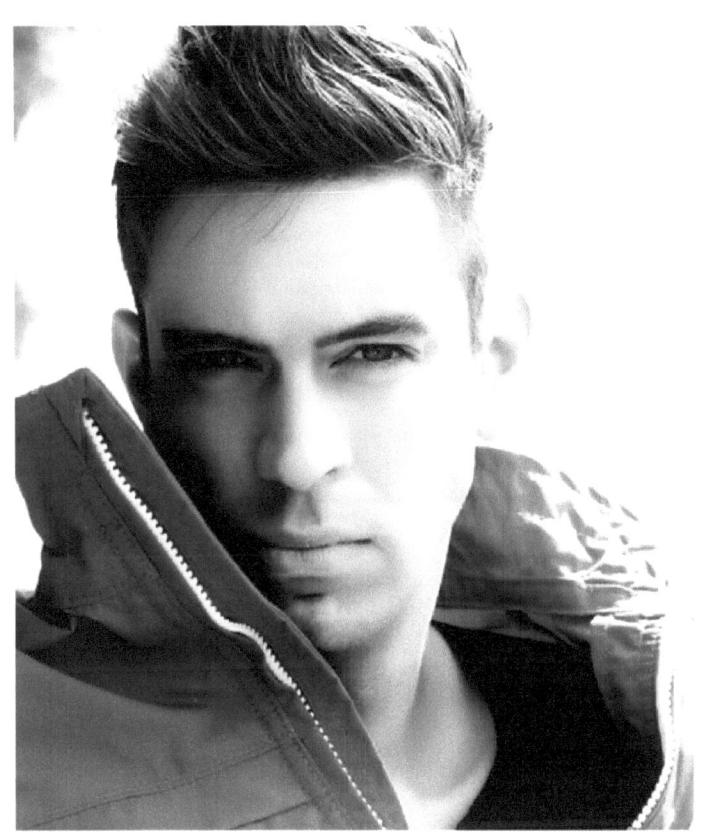

Negative Space

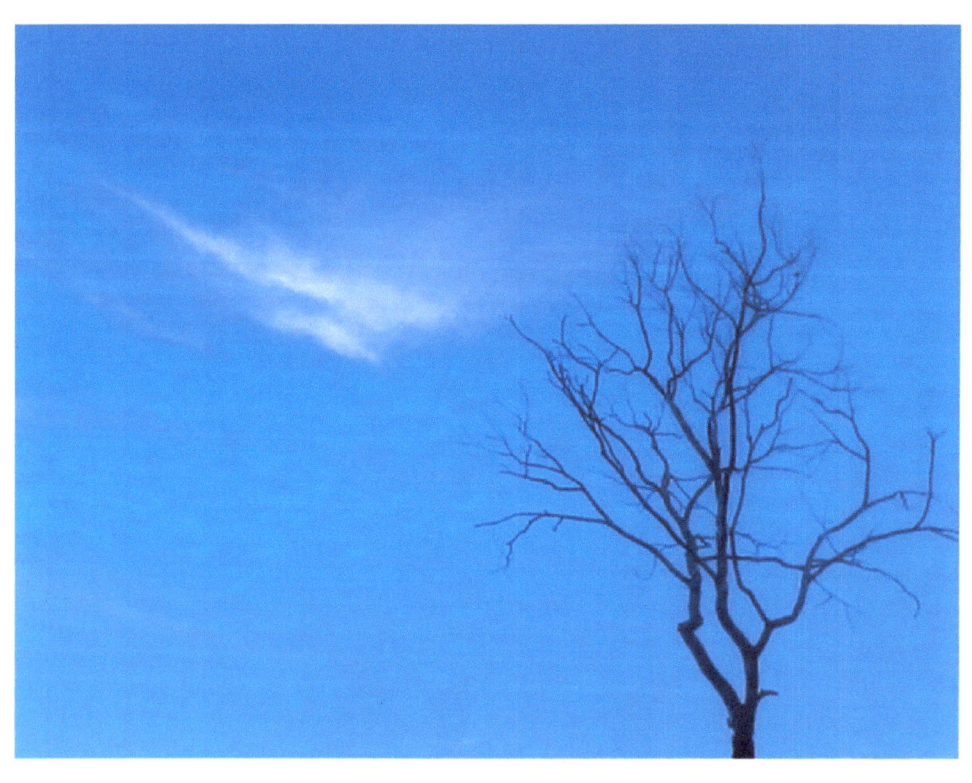

Conclusion

Rekindling your passion, starting your hobby or launching your career in photography has never become more possible when you are fully knowledgeable on the art and the use of the camera. Remember, photography is not learned overnight. In fact, most photographers, even the experienced ones, will say that every day and every photo are opportunities to learn and discover something new. While you may be able to read this guide in one sitting, learning photography and its tools will sure to prompt you to go back and re-read the contents of this guide.

After reading this book, experience will take over as your guide, it is the best teacher after all. Never be afraid in tinkering with your camera or experimenting with your photography. When you travel unexplored territory or in this case use something that may not be completely familiar to you, there is where true learning takes place. In the end you must be patient in your learning and be open to new and exciting opportunities to enhance your photography skills.

If you are a beginner or relatively new in photography, it is highly recommended that you start slowly but surely. Photography is for everybody but only those that are patient, brave and most importantly creative can truly become experts in this worthwhile endeavor. The journey towards mastery in photography, as long as it may be, starts with a single step. Take that overlooked camera from your shelf now, start taking photographs wherever and whenever you want. There is no specific time or place to take the best photos. With your skills and knowledge, every place and every time will be the best.

www.ingramcontent.com/pod-product-compliance
Lightning Source LLC
Chambersburg PA
CBHW040850180526
45159CB00001B/374